# Silk Dress

*poems by*

# Lydia Chang

*Finishing Line Press*
Georgetown, Kentucky

# Silk Dress

*For Norman*

*And in memory of my mother*

## ACKNOWLEDGMENTS

These poems first appeared in the following publications:

"Smith-Corona XL1000," *All Ways A Woman* (Staten Island: The College of Staten Island, 1989)
"A Backyard Tree," "A Lonely Requiem," "Mother as a Drummer," "Statistics of Error," "Targeting Japanese Betties," "You Break, You Take," *QOTC Newscap* (Creative Corner, 1990)
"Medical Love," *Life Line* (1989)
"Corns on My Toes," "In Flushing," "Silk Dress," *Newtown Literary* (June, 2015)
"A Lilac Sweater," "A Bowl of Rice," *Pearl Port* (1989)

Publisher: Leah Maines
Editor: Christen Kincaid
Cover Art: The Moon Goddess Chang E, www.metmuseum.org, (CC0 1.0)
Author Photo: Norman Stock
Cover Design: Elizabeth Maines McCleavy

Printed in the USA on acid-free paper.
Order online: www.finishinglinepress.com
also available on amazon.com

Author inquiries and mail orders:
Finishing Line Press
P. O. Box 1626
Georgetown, Kentucky 40324
U. S. A.

# Table of Contents

## Silk Dress
*(After Tiananmen Square)*

I walked out of an ancient Chinese drawing
wearing an ancient pink dress,
printed with red peonies.
Pure silk,
whose silk-worms were fed by young maidens' hands,
whose cocoons were unwound by their hands,
whose cloth was woven by hands,
whose flowers were embroidered by hands,
stitches finished by hand.

The dress, wrapped on my body,
was soft, light and breathable
I was the Moon-Goddess floating down from heaven.

I longed for that dress.
It rippled as if breathing.
I embraced and caressed it,
I wanted to possess it.
I would have, but as I stood in Tiananmen Square
I smelled gun-powder on the dress,
and saw blood dripping from the hands that created it.

## Corns on My Toes

Sharply elevated,
stubbornly-hardened, slightly transparent
grain-sized corns on both little toes.
Quite strategically grown,
they cause me to limp even when I wear
Gucci shoes.
So I take up filing.
Using a $2.59 flint stone file, I sit on my toilet cover,
left foot resting on my right knee,
the left hand grabbing the left foot,
I fix my eyes on the left toe.
If the corn has given me a hard time that day
I file it harshly, ferociously, cold-bloodedly.
From time to time, I tap the file on the faucet handle.
It gives me pleasure to see my own skin
return to dust,
dispersed in the running water like a balmy powder.
I am dying a small peaceful death.

One month later,
I feel the little corns start to irritate me again.
I am shocked and surprised, but somewhat relieved,
to see part of my body still growing.

## One Billion Chinese and One

For two months
I've been lying on the bed, on the sofa, on the armchair
to keep my feet off the ground.
A life gestating for the third time
in my body.
After two mischances,
how fervently I pray
it will mature and blossom!

My husband has become more amorous and aroused,
touching my tummy endearingly and anxiously.
But something inside me
is pushing, compulsively.
A little spasm,
and I was soon sitting in a pool of blood,
half fainting, semi-conscious.

Suddenly, telephone ringing,
a call from Joe, his cousin
announcing the birth of his son.
His one hand held the receiver, quivering,
the other hand wiping his wet sticky face,
crying, not even holding his tears back.

"My gynecologist explained to me
miscarriages happen when the fetus is not healthy,"
I whispered apologetically.

> Each word from his twisted mouth
> came with deliberation and clarity:
> "I want a child,
> to bear my name,
> to hand my name down.
> I want to see you give birth to a child
> even if it is defective or disabled."

> He left the room,
> and slammed the front door
> shaking the house.

I was left with that pool of blood
and a messy fetus, only a piece of wrinkled skin.
"As if there's nothing in me
that's dead also."
Lee, Chang, Wong, Poo.... a billion of them,
common as sand,
what's one less.

Slowly and firmly, I walked to the phone,
and called the doctor myself.

## A Lilac Sweater

Today she bought a pair of knitting needles,
five lilac colored spools of angora yarn,
and started to knit again,
for her only daughter's 50th birthday.

Years ago, newly married,
because it was his first born,
he commanded her to knit the layettes, insisting
knitting was virtuous motherhood.

Lilac, her favorite color,
she chose for the yarn.
She loved the color so much
that her dreams were lilac.
But he made her change the yarn to blue:
a beacon for the birth of an heir.

How she knitted
every precious
second away, her life in every stitch.
Youth, vitality, beauty...
Keats, Mme. Curie, Tanhauser, Monet,
    Chopin...
Curiosity and Civilization,
once the walls of a university
closed behind her.

Her young agile hand, knitting,
a complete layette,
a truncated dream.
The child has outgrown the knitted gown,
the tiny cap cast into wasteland.

In the later half of her life
she picks up her unfulfilled future
but  has never picked up a
needle or yarn.

Today, face wrinkled,
hand deformed by arthritis,
she knits a sweater, the color of lilac, with gusto.

## Targeting Japanese Betties

*(During the Sino-Japanese War)*

The Mitsubishi G4M Japanese Bombers, called Betties, are flying over my
    head;
their thundering noise penetrates my heart-beat, raises my blood-pressure,
tears my 3,000 ear receptors into pieces.
I see the head of each pilot: eyes, nose, and mouth.
Had I an anti-aircraft machine-gun,
I would shoot through their eyes,
like Halloween masks pierced by metal hooks in a store.

My mother, in her pastel nightgown,
standing near my bed,
woke me gently from a shrieking air-raid siren.
She did not want to wake me earlier
so that I could get more sleep before school.
Like an angel and a rock, smiling,
she hurried me with knapsack, food and water,
lifted me in mid air,
and ran breaking through traffic lights,
my eyes still half open.

Roaring over-head, those cursed Japanese Betties, plunging so low
the pilots were looking at me and my mother with sadistic glee.
Two steps from the shelter door,
I heard a grating twang of their bombing right behind my back.
Strong hands grabbed my mother and me
and dragged us inside the cave-like gate.
The whistling explosion of the dropped bomb
was more deafening than an earthquake,
Jolting everyone inside.

When it was over, our house was just 2 inches of debris.
I found a family picture and
one of my silver-inlaid chopsticks uninjured.

I was evacuated—abroad, forever.
Tonight, looking at the only family picture before going to bed,
I shoot those damned Japanese Betties
One by one with my inlaid silver chopstick.

## This Chinese Tea Is Stale

Tea for two and two for tea,
a girl for you and a boy for me.
…………………………………………...

He made her knit
all sweaters in blue,
and sew all pillow cases, bed-sheets…in blue.
Buy the layettes in blue
because his mother had told him
even if she had intercourse with her husband's foot,
it would be a boy. It runs in the family blood.

After labor, a frail little bundle of
red face and thick black hair
in blue. A girl. A replica of her father.
Dejected, despondent, ashamed,
He refused to look at and hold and talk to
both females
in the midst of celebration and congratulations.

Five years elapsed.
Father was holding a banquet
for one hundred guests.
A more robust, slightly larger bundle in blue,
fair and beautiful. A replica of his mother.
Father exhibited the infant boy, like a prize prey,
To the guests, one by one.
"Se mira, no se toca." (One can look at him, but not touch him.)

At home, father told a piece of his mind to the baby girl,
"Even your brother's foot is born with a
better shape than yours."
This tea is as stale as
the history of Chinese boys favored,
girls devalued.

## In Flushing

Hurrying away through a busy street
I was interrupted by a timid hand,
with several strands of beads hanging from it.

Turning my eyes from the hand to the face,
I saw a woman
in Chinese coat and pantaloons.

She was murmuring
"Check it out, Miss."

She could have been my mother:
uprooted and humiliated
by her loss of independence,
my mother would put up a stand,
selling something
to make a few dollars
in order to buy back one ounce of her dignity.

"Check it out,
check it out..." echoing like innuendo
in my ears, in my heart.

## Medical Love

Like an injection with a hypodermic needle,
it rubs a little, pinches a little, hurts a little, swells a little.
When the fluid goes into the body,
even the wound disappears, and you are healed.
Who can Rx it with the right prescription?

It is like myopia.
It cannot see far, and it cannot see clearly.
It has to be corrected with glasses.
Suddenly, it opens the eyes and it needs glasses forever.
Does love do better with 20-20 vision?

It is like a transplant.
You are dying to have it.
It encounters rejection instantly.
The more rejection it receives, the more drugs it needs.
At the end, either it conquers the rejection,
or it is rejected by the receiver.

It is like continuous ambulatory peritoneal dialysis.
It is carried inside the body,
being cherished four times a day with TLC.
You depend on it for life.
Although you know someone is grateful that you were created,
you are replaceable when you are worn out, like a lost kidney.
(Isn't medical technology wonderful?)

(Big sigh!)
It is like acupuncture.
Like anything Chinese, exotic and inexplicable,
to those who believe, it cures;
to those who do not, it won't.
Since the needles do not contain any substance,
you feel several pinches, but it does no harm.
Shortly after, the stings enter into oblivion.

## The Saints Are Ordinary People

He kissed her good-bye.
She, on her way to church on All Saints' Day,
He, looking for donut holes for breakfast and
a newspaper for his day.

After 15 minutes,
the donut waitress did not serve him.
"Damn her," he said impatiently,
and stomped out of the coffee shop.
"I'm going to make my own coffee."
He bought the 8 pound paper, returned to her apartment,
and with an assured precision, hit the lock with a key.
Deftly, hard, dexterously he tried.
But the key could not penetrate the lock.
Then he tried another key, and another,
All five keys ended with miserable disappointment.
"It's impossible to open the door!
She's deliberately given me the wrong key!
I'll go to the church, drag her from
the audience, yell at her and get
the right keys from her,"
he said with a vengeance.

At the church he couldn't find her.
The pastor was just preaching,
"The Saints are ordinary people,"
then announced there was no coffee hour.
He spewed the usual vehement curses,
stomped out of the church,
and wandered three hours on the street.
Sitting on a wet bench,
standing on a damp street corner,
hungry, starving, furious, he fumed,
"This relationship is not working."

When she came back,
she used the same keys he'd just tried,
and precisely, with one turn,
opened the door.

## A Bowl of Rice

As I prepared to throw away the leftover bowl of rice
a sharp pang started in my chest.
Grasping the pail,
my hands trembling, I put this pail of rice
into the refrigerator with reverence!
"How much I wish I could give this bowl of rice
to my mother!"

My mother whom I have not seen for decades,
from the time when she was running from my brother's house
   in darkness.
Like an abandoned child, she was crying and staggering,
"I am hungry!
I have not had enough rice to eat."
Because the rice was rationed in China,
my sister-in-law locked her food in a closet,
and my mother's meals were reduced to two per day.
She could not care less about any revolution;
she wanted only a bowl of rice
which was her birthright.

I was two oceans away from my mother.
Had I known, I would have taken a
bowl of rice with both hands
flying across the waters,
even under the death penalty,
to offer a bowl of rice, white steaming fragrant rice
to my mother.

## A Backyard Tree

This healthy and loaded tree came with the house.
I had no intention of buying or owning a tree
because my house is right across from Kissena Park.
But this tree, with its roots half-way exposed on the ground
had already penetrated
the little backyard patio from underneath.
It might uproot my house someday.
So I cut a few branches
to show Linda, a botanist at the Nature Center.
It was a silver maple,
capable of growing 2 to 4 feet in diameter
and 40 to 80 feet high.
"The tree's life is about 40 years,
then it will slowly die, " she said.

A sadness crept over me.
I have lived all over the world surrounded by trees
but have not seen one single dying tree yet,
not because the trees in my life didn't die,
it is because I myself have been so rootless
and have not lived in one spot long enough
to accompany a tree dying.
Now that I have seen this tree sprout,
grow green leaves,
bloom and blossom,
I want to settle down here.
But do I really want to see this tree wither and decay?

**Smith-Corona XL 1000**

I need a new typewriter:
To type my dissertation on Chinese male impotence,
My research project on how to be a successful homeless lady,
My District School Board member campaign flyers,
My rebuttal to the full-of-black-lies evaluation for my tenure,
My full-of-white-lies employment application letters,
Jazzed up recommendation references for friends,
Documents for my divorce from a manic-depressive psychiatrist husband,
    who had summoned State Troopers to have me committed to a mental
    hospital—by a hair's breadth miss,
Personal classified ad for blind dates,
Answers to dating services—to a bereaved Hassidic gentleman with 16 kids,
Who wanted me to shave my hair and wear a wig instead, and who insisted
    that from Chinese to Hebrew was simply a stone's throw away.
To type corrections on bank statements, Visa card statements, telephone
    statements, Con-Ed statements, transcript statements,
Statements to police precincts for being mugged, robbed and pick-pocketed.
Request for Phil Donahue Show's materials—how to achieve peaceful
    involvement with mother, daughter and siblings, and peaceful
    uninvolvement with friends, lovers and ex-husband, to refute or support
    him on some vital issues.
Letters to dear Abby and Ann Landers, to Walt Disneyland.
To type angry letters—righteously so—to Macys for the return of a piece of
    wrongly delivered furniture, the overpayment for it, and the overcharge
    for it.
Urgent letter to the IRS for my erroneous Social Security Number, and for
    their over-taxing me.
Letters to some senator to support "Insane but guilty" convictions, and asking
    help for a crack on my wall.
To AT & T for nightly obscene phone calls,
To my local Councilwoman to intervene and stop a neighbor's dog barking in
    the middle of the night,
And to control scattered garbage bags not collected by nearby restaurants,
    secreting nauseating fish odors which made me unable to taste fish for
    three whole months;
To deal with a homeless man bruised, but apparently dozing off snugly under
    the sun at the street corner.
To the Director of the Queen's Botanical Garden because some well-attired,
    but undisciplined children did not keep off the lawn,
To the New York Times to protest that one of its Gourmet recipes did not
    taste good,

To type my poems, my fantasies,
My unfinished song pieces;
To type my memories from far away and long ago
Which have diminished almost into a  hazy smoke
Twirling like a whirlwind into a nowhere somewhere.


I want a new electronic typewriter,
Because the first one, a manual Hermes, was a blackmailed gift
When I threatened splitting-up.
But looking at newspaper advertisement's HELP columns, for days,
Simply to find out that I was good for nothing,
Even as a maid.
That I had always had,
And I had not had to do any of the above,
For most of it was being done for me.
I embraced the little, feather-light and portable Hermes,
Frantically moved my inexperienced fingers,
Accompanied by a self-study manual,
I carried it to type in parks while my children were sliding from the toboggan,
Typed in the kitchen, while burning some filet mignon,
Typed on the table while the children were eating and fighting,
Typed on the night-table while they were sleeping,
Typed on my knees while my daughter was playing Scarlatti on her piano, and
    complained our rhythms were not synchronized,
Typed, staring blankly at the goldfish, and with tears streaming down my face
    due to the pending divorce,
My year old son wiped off my tears with a handkerchief, whispering manfully
    in my ears, "Daddy is treating you better now,"
Typed in the car while we were traveling, racing behind the Shah's deposed
    Empress, Soroya, on the way to Biarritz,
Typed on the boat at the Tigre Lake in Madrid while my children were rowing,
In Barcelona watching a bullfight,
In Mont Blanc while riding the funiculars up,
In Las Islas de Majorca visiting Georges Sand's and Chopin's love nest,
Almost typing while paying homage in the Sistine Chapel, but was hushed by
    a venerable looking monk,
Yet did get to type in the nursery while my children were attending their
    Sunday School.
After 3 months, I exited.

The Smith-Corona XL 1000 is my reality,
I am now alone and keep typing.

## Peach-Colored Cheongsam (Long-Gown)

I decided to shop for a new dress for my daughter's wedding.
Shopping for clothing I do purely out of necessity.
    During my school days in China,
    I wore a light-blue uniform all year round,
        simplicity personified.

But this summer, in order to recuperate physically from broken wrists
and financially from workers' meager compensation,
I worked overtime and accumulated a big fat check of $1,000.
Walking along the Main Street,
I saw windows displaying peach colors.

"My first peach-colored cheongsam," I murmured,
which my mother had made for me
to be introduced to an adult society
of Confucian dogma and Christian commandments.
The dress, with one inch of hard collar to make my neck numb
and a long slit cut to expose part of my bony legs,
did not make me willowy but Twiggyish.

It was a balmy, early summer evening.
A party for families of four generations.
And I was walking around, alone and lonely,
when a teenage boy suddenly appeared.
He gawked at me as if we had never seen each other before,
yet we had just fought over an idiotic hopscotch game.
I had chased after him around the block,
caught him and poured a jar of water on his head
right on that spot where he was now gazing at me.
"Gee, you've changed," he said,
peeking down at his own sneakers and running away.

Confused, I wanted to listen to the music, dance and scream.
But then a young man swept me around
in his arms,
leading me to the tune of a waltz.
Dancing to the melody, I felt ecstatic,
while trying not to step on his toes.
Abruptly a matron
sandwiched between us, leading me away.
"Young lady, you were dancing too close to that man.

In social dance etiquette, you should only lean on his arms,
and keep the lower part of your body a distance from his."
She was my widowed aunt,
who perpetually wore black.
After that, colorful dresses never found their way to my closets.

My daughter took me to the Saks Fifth Avenue's Teen Department.
for her bridal gown.
A delicate brocade dress, with soft peach-color flower designs,
a V-cut neckline in princess style,
hung on the rack, unnoticed.
The salesgirl smiled, and nodded, saying:
"This gown will fit you perfectly as a bridesmaid."
Amused, I tried it on.

Coming out from the fitting room,
and facing a larger than life-size mirror,
 I was transformed.
In that instant, my years of spotless inhibition
were ejected into the clouds;
my femininity resuscitated from ash.
I bought the dress,
and wore it in a rage.

**You Break, You Take**

Shopping in a variety store
For cheap imported crystal items,
I was struck with a hand-written card in red ink:
"Stop helping yourself.
   You break,
   You take."

How many people practice what they preach?
One night-stands: You take it, you break it.

Unconsummated marriages: They take it, they don't break it.

Couples living together: They half take it, they half break it.

Fractured marriages: They totally take it, they totally break it.

Prolonged affairs: They break it, they don't take it.

Blind dates: You don't take it, you don't break it.

Romeo and Juliet: They never take it, they absolutely break it.

Goethe's Young Werther: He meant to take it, he's unsure about breaking it.

Mid Summer Night's Dream: They are confused about taking it, they are
   confused about breaking it.

There I was in the variety store
Facing an ugly vase for a single flower,
Touching with trembling hands not to break it,
Or else I would have to take it.

## Statistics of Error

Numbers.
Bell shapes.
Continuum.
Average.
2,000,000 marriages.
300,000 POOSLT (People Of Opposite Sex Living Together)
One out of two marriages ended in divorce.

You are young and fresh,
like a deep red rosebud,
chased by a whirlwind of butterflies and bees.
You have rejected the most ardent and the most true.
You have committed the Type I Error: a hypothesis may be rejected
when it is true.
Looking around, you have gone through a whole lot with life and with him,
the wedding bells are ringing,
you have nodded to his proposal.
Lo! Type II Error: a hypothesis may be accepted when it is false.

What is the probability in love?

## Have it, Have it Not

After our ephemeral poetry reading,
we were offered a free ride to the City,
even though we would miss the moonlight
on blossom-covered pavement
and our allergy.
Crammed in the car to full capacity,
we were alerted by the driver:
"There is a safety belt for everyone in the back seat.
Put them on."

Norman started to fumble.
I have it.
I don't have it.
Do you have it?
Thank goodness, at least you have it.
Now I lost it,
I don't have it any more.
Damn it, I had it.
Help me to get it.
Well, I have the tip of it
but I can't put it in.
Damn it,
I lost it again.
Well, so much for now.
Maybe I'll try later.

Amidst his 'having it and not having it'
the car sped on.

## A Lonely Requiem

*(In memory of Dean Wang Wen-Tien, who was the Dean of a Chinese girl's High School)   2001*

When the air-raid siren sounded
we, the sinless, crimeless bunch
grabbed our school bags and ran,
to a shelter,
or to an open plain,
looking at the bright sky
and counting the stars.
When Red Water flooded,
the same sinless, crimeless bunch
were herded to a prison cell,
chased to a rural farm,
the ceiling gloomy,
and no stars to count.

50 years on the east side of the Ocean,
and 50 years on the west side of the Ocean,
you, our Dean, spent your ages here, wise, unbent, feisty,
alone and lonely.
Like the rest of the sinless, crimeless bunch,
hopes half accomplished, wishes half fulfilled,
dead and dying,
your remains squeezed into an urn,
not a single handful of our soil to bury you with.
Rest in peace!
Our beloved Dean!

**Amnesia**

You thought you had fled from the blood,
the lice,
the constant storming open of the door,
the slogans…
to a meandering thousand island.
Until one humid and steaming afternoon,
after taking out a collection of 14 letters
written between 20 long years
but dragging as if a lifetime
here are the words written by my father
like his remains after cremation
crushed all together in an envelope.

**Driving**

love is like driving a car
to avoid a crash
you have to take hints
from nonverbal cues
a blinking signal
a waving of a hand
the raising of an eyebrow
an understanding nod
a stern stare
a shrugging of shoulders
a wild scream
you either lead
or follow the signals

## On My Treadmill

I tread, tread, tread
on the mill,
inclined.
I'm treading uphill.
Then I see something on the windowsill,
like a star signaling from far away,
 silent and still as a statuette
as if the sky, the earth, the clock, and I myself
have been forever
standing there still.

**Flute Practice**

finishing the scales
I took the flute apart
looking inside its heart
to cleanse it
a big teardrop
was floating there
I sighed
not up to the standard yet

## Saturday Lunch Special

we talk about the evening we met
the conversation of the first minutes
the argument of the first hour
the location of the first dinner
the dishes of our first entrée
the offering of his first desert—which I declined
meeting with family members
the first wonderful night we were really close
sharing triumphs disappointments, disillusion, anger,
    satisfaction
......................................................................................
an order of garlic bread, my favorite, is served
he reminds me not to eat two pieces
just one
because "you are allergic to butter"
but he does not remember a hundred items
that he cannot eat because of his diet restrictions

## Disappearing in Twin-Beds

For years
I smelled his special scent
and he sniffed the fragrance
from my soap or cream
he said I tickled him
but he touched me as if attacking
from nowhere
I sensed him, like a hurricane
he heard my heaving breath like a sleeping dog

we suffered from Intimate Sleeping Disorder

we bought a set of twin-beds
separate but together
we have slept soundly since then.
silence. we sleep soundly
disappearing in twin-beds

## Culture Gap

Friends from the PRC appeared in this nation
to meet
after 4 decades of non-communication
for a picnic.
Friends, when last seen, who were just reaching
puberty,
now have passed through their middle-age crisis.
Friends, living in the opposite direction of
the Pacific Ocean,
are meeting through grapevine connections,
who used to live just a couple of blocks away.
Profound distances of ideology, politics, sociology, linguistics and
Time!
have corroded their similarities.
Forget about those differences,
let's get together and have fun, like we did before.


We took
paper cups, paper plates,
throwaway chopsticks;
                    they brought plastic forks and spoons.
We carried precooked Chinese buns, dumplings
right from a steamer.
                    They had prepared hamburgers, hot-dogs,
                    boiled Virginia ham cold cuts, hard salami,
                    complete with ketchup and mustard,
                    displayed as if from a caterer.
We ordered turnip cake, roasted duckling
(the one hanging in a Cantonese restaurant's windows),
smoked chicken feet (called phoenix craws in a fancy Chinese restaurant).
                    They offered barbecued steak, baked potato with sour
cream, knishes and pieces of pizza.

We brought almond-jello for desert.
                    They presented us an ice-cream angel cake
                    delicately boxed as if for a birthday.
It was a hardship for a few chubby dieting Chinese to smell it,
but declining it would mean an outright offense
according to 5000 years of Chinese civilization.

It was a surprise and a shock to everyone:
the authentic Chinese and the banana Chinese
(white inside but yellow outside),
but we smiled at each other, delighted at
each others' good intentions.
They thought we had acquired an Americanized stomach.
We were secretly angry that they had not
brought with them the best food we could have
prepared by the cook
whom they had brought with them from China.

## On Becoming Beautiful

the excitement when informed of a fresh kidney
after years of tubes
fasting
lack of appetite
high protein
low protein
pasticcio
hard labor
perseverance
he is told by all of the
doctors:
Beautiful:
the kidney is beautiful!
a post kidney transplant diagnosis.

the excitement when informed of a fresh kidney
disappointment if the kidney's not matching
the patience of watching calling waiting
the kidney weakened
creatinine rising to 8, 9
one more, a summons to Death
possible Hell, a fathomless hole

then one morning
totally out of expectation
a nurse called
"a kidney, it's thought to be your perfect match"
we called a cab
met it's experienced driver, 65 years old
driving extra-cautiously with each inch
to exchange the old, diseased and ugly kidney for a new and strong one

as he was wheeled to the operating room
the surgeon, holding the kidney for transplantation
describing it as if it was a hunted treasure
"it's young, strong, well-preserved, beautiful"
and the patient trailed off to slumber

after three hours
he was out on a stretcher
Susan and I were waiting outside

as the doctor announced
"well done, a success, he's urinating normally"
Susan, seeing him on the stretcher
half awakened from the surgery
exclaimed loudly, clapping hands
Beautiful, Beautiful!
instantly he opened his eyes, sparkling
"Who? the kidney or me?"

### Seven Year Itch...In Remission
*(For Norman's transplant anniversary)*

Life was rescued
Birth
Dialysis
From a kidney transplant
Blessed be the donor!
A young man dead from a gunshot
But his kidney
A treasure, a blessing
jumping and breathing
implanted in me
like a pearl implanted in an oyster
painful but living
priceless, miraculous!
medications, diets, shots, doctors, minor surgeries,
with TLC
my worthy kidney
does his job for me.

Seven years!
Like a normal human being,
I should be stimulated by some itch!
At my marital bliss,
I don't feel a thing
Acute pain and preservation have been my reality!
As for those mundane pleasures (matters, issues)
Let me kick them into remission!

## Broken and Bound Feet

"O la la, do the next one,
O la la, do the next one,"
One by one, he did it.
He gently performs the prescribed strokes on her feet
plaster recently removed
ossification of a fractured ankle completed.
It felt good for both of them,
the massager and the massagee.
"Do you think Chinese men could feel titillated
massaging his wife's broken feet?" Half talking to herself,
she suddenly remembered a tragic-comic story.

*         *         *

For some time, Chinese society was measured by
the contrast of a family's status against its females' feet.
The higher and nobler the class of the family
the smaller the size and the more bent their females' feet.
This was the story my mother told:

"Born just a few years
prior to the collapse of the last dynasty,
my young tender chubby feet were destined to be
bound, deformed, bent and broken
right where the middle arch was
as early as 3 years old
before the soft bone hardens into a solid bone.
        My mother, raised by feudal commandments,
ordered the maid
to have my feet bound.
Thirty yards by three inches width
of pure white silk,
was wound round, round, and round one foot.
Then another foot, wound by pure white silk,
round, round and round by another 30 yards by three inches of pure white
    silk.
        Then they sprinkled salty water on the feet.
Heartless, motionless, was my mother.
Heartless, full of motion was the maid.
In one hour, a fun-loving four year old,

an active child
became a motionless Lorelei
crying, lying on the floor
crippled, unable to stand up, refusing to stand on my feet,
nothing could move these stony-hearted women.
It felt like
a million sharpened needles cutting through
my skin, my muscle, my tendons, my ligaments and my bones.
         A stocky man broke into the room,
'Get out all of you,
I will deal with it.' He yelled; but with poise.
Using a pair of scissors,
he efficiently cut the thread, cut open the yards of silk,
unto the last layer.
My little feet were set free again.
I jumped, stood up and
bowed to that powerful man,
'He was my father.'
Females waiting in the hall thought
He had calmed me down and
rocked me to sleep.
Quietly they left.
The next morning, a sleeping
baby girl was found in her bed
amidst yards of white silk
in shredded pieces spread around her.
Water and salt on the floor,
it was a messy scene.

My mother was alerted, and called in.
This time, she wept.
'My daughter's marriage, her future
has been ruined by this
uncultivated and uncivilized man.
How can I ever face the world
marrying out a
big-footed low-class village domestic
daughter of mine?' she wailed.
Motionlessly, she ordered
the maids to execute once again the
wrapping, the silk, the salty water

furiously.
Came the dusk,
came the night,
I was rescued again.
This ritual went on for years.
The yards of silk must have been able to
wrap around the earth many times over!
Until I was 15, I had a reputation for
playing hopscotch
with brothers and male cousins outdoors,
because my feet were slim and small,
but not broken and bent."

She knew
her ankles were going
to heal and become strong
because she knew
she had unbroken and unbent
blood in her veins.

## Mother as a Drummer

The first violinist gave the tune.
The director mounted the podium,
baton in his hand,
more stylish than Fred Astaire's stick,
accepting the applause with an elegant bow.
The prima donna curtsied
triumphantly to the clapping hands.
Pavarotti and his Amour drank to them
only with each others' eyes,
and the audience stamped their feet.

In the dark, furthest corner,
behind two cymbals, a gong
and two drums
stood the drummer.
He was intense, totally immersed
in the music, yet restrained.
He could only play to his heart's delight
if he was needed.
Often he was called upon
with the slightest signal from the baton.
Yet, without a drummer,
the 1812 Overture would become
an Unfinished Symphony.

I heard
my daughter sing to me:
Watch, listen (Regard! Ecoute)
Step aside, stay behind.
 Let me do my own thing. (Permite-moi faire mes affaires.)
(And with her coloratura cadenza)
Rescue! A-I-D-E-Z  M-O-I!

Her voice mingled with the drumroll
making a magnificent grand finale.